COMMUNISM AND HUMAN VALUES

Communism and Human Values

by

MAURICE CORNFORTH

INTERNATIONAL PUBLISHERS *New York*

Contents

Note

This essay on *Communism and Human Values* reproduces, with some slight changes, three chapters from my *Marxism and the Linguistic Philosophy*, first published in 1965. References originally made to views of "linguistic" philosophers have been deleted, and, for the sake of rounding this off as an independent essay, some small additions have been made and some re-arrangement of the original material.

London, August 1971   M. C.

1

Human Society

"What is man?" is the key question which men have to answer for themselves, and in terms of it manage their lives. Marxism is essentially an attempt to answer it.

Men are distinguished from all other forms of life on earth by their social production of their material means of life. The natural precondition was the evolution of the human hands and brain, which led to men distinguishing themselves from the rest of nature by their social use of tools and speech—by working and speaking, living by labour and, in so doing, developing the capacity to imagine and to think.

Homo sapiens is the product of the evolution of species by natural selection. But with men living by social production a new kind of evolutionary development begins. In general, the evolutionary development of living species amounts to change in means and methods of appropriating the organism's requirements from nature. Prior to man, this has always meant some structural change in organisms themselves; for instance, forms of life which evolved in the sea gave rise to those living on land through the development of lungs. With men, however, the organic structure does not change, but in the course of social production men develop techniques. For instance, men can now fly, not because they have grown wings but because they have built aircraft; and they have acquired remarkable powers of sight, not because the structure of the eyes has changed, but because they have built microscopes and telescopes.

Human evolution is the evolution of techniques. And it is a progress, in as much as, in a most obvious sense, men advance from lower to higher techniques. Further, this progress is, in a sense, predetermined from the very beginning of social production—not that every technique was bound to be discovered by a certain time, or to be discovered at all, but that in the relation of the human organism to nature, though still unexplored by man, is contained the possibility of every technique that can ever be discovered, and the dependence of the more complex and later techniques on the simpler and earlier ones.

Living by social production, men develop the tools and implements they use for production, together with the knowledge and skill involved in using them. In short, they develop their forces of production. And to do this, they enter into relations with one another necessary to ensure the performance of labour, the management of the whole productive process and the distribution of the product. In short, they enter into social relations of production. And the progressive development of forces of production brings in turn changes in relations of production and so in the whole structure and character of human society.

The hypothesis which Marx put forward as the fundamental law governing social life (and it has yet to be falsified or replaced by one that fits all the facts better) consisted of positing, first, that people in society have always to bring their relations of production into conformity with their forces of production, and second, that the relations of production condition the character of all human institutions and human activities and purposes. Without production men cannot live as men, and without conformable relations of production they cannot successfully produce. The existence of given relations of production is, then, the basis on which the whole of social life is carried on; and whenever, in the development of social production, relations of production have ceased to conform with the developing forces of production, that is, have ceased to promote their successful use but begun to disrupt it, then they have to be brought back into conformity.

2

Human Relations

All human relations develop out of the social production of the material means of life. Indeed, human individuals themselves are so created, since it is only by being brought up a member of society, and so entering into human relations and experiencing human needs, that the organism genetically constituted as *Homo sapiens* becomes a person.

By "human relations" is meant not simply any relation into which human individuals enter, but those relations into which only human individuals, or persons, can enter. For instance, just to sit down together, or to go hunting together, is not a specifically human relation; but to sit down at a meeting or a party, or to go hunting after the manner of a primitive tribe, or with the Pytchley or Quorn, is a human relation—only people could participate in such relationships. The uniqueness of man lies in the social use of tools and speech, the latter being requisite for the former. Human relations develop among tool-using animals, but they are not confined to relations of production and their distinctive mark is the way language enters into them.

The use of language is an essential element in the formation of human relations. They could not exist unless spoken into existence.

Thus, for example, the use of words in the marriage ceremony marries people; the words serve not merely to state that certain people are married, but to marry them. But quite apart from such uses of words essential for the conduct of human institutions, the very capacity of language to express propositions means that by using it people bring themselves into relationships which could not hold apart from its use; and these are the uniquely *human* relations.

When uses of language are thus understood, a certain

mystery that has often been attributed to human relations is dissipated. They have been supposed to be in some way "transcendental", because they seem to elude any merely naturalistic description of observable facts and material motion. Describe all the manifold physical and chemical motions of human bodies, and you have still said nothing about human relations. But human bodies do not enter into human relations independently of what they say and think, so that language has more to do with these relations than simply to state them as facts. It is only by using language that people enter into them.

Thus if observers from another planet were to carry home any adequate account of what they found people doing, they would have not only to observe and record their behaviour but discover the meaning of human speech.

Indeed, language is an essential means whereby human individuals relate themselves to the external world in ways additional to those of other animals. Men obtain their requirements from nature by the purposive social use of tools and implements, and this they can only do in so far as language serves them for the imaginative conception of their purpose and for organising its realisation. In this process, whatever affects men is translated into terms of human thought, reflected and related to other things in terms of the categories of human thought, and thus becomes an object of human knowledge. By this means men relate themselves to nature in another way than the other animals. And so do they relate themselves to each other. Hence every relation between persons, whether a production relation or not, and whether an institutionalised type of relation or not, owes its existence to the use of language.

Take love, for example. Does this consist simply of mutual feelings, a purely emotional bond which can come into existence independently of people's possessing the use of language? Absolutely dumb sexual attachment would not be human, and it is well known that the whole character of such attachment between persons involves the exercise of imagination and varies with the way they have learned to think of each other. It is not merely that feelings may be expressed in language, but that human feelings are not felt by animals lacking the use of language, since without language they lack imagination and could not enter into human relationships. (This example provides a clue, incidentally, to the role which literature plays in developing human relations; the expression it gives to them and the images it makes of them are factors in making and changing them.)

The use of language owes its origin to social production, since to carry on social production people must speak to one another. And just as social production is the distinctive activity of man, so are relations of production, or property relations, the basic human relations. They are the precondition of all other human relations, which are all conditioned by whatever are the forms of property. All relations into which people enter are so conditioned—how people treat one another, how they regard each other, how they co-operate together and how they fight one another.

Not the least important of the uses of language, then, is to constitute or bring into being the relations of production. Marx already equated these with "property relations", calling the latter "but a legal expression of the same thing". Words are, of course, used to describe property—as when one says that a large part of the land on which London is built is the property of the Duke of Westminster. But the use of words is also requisite to institute property.

Animals which do not *say* "These things are ours", or "This is mine" and "This is yours", have no property. A dog may guard its bone and a Duke his land; but the land belongs to the Duke in another sense than the bone to the dog; property begins with appropriation (collective or individual), but does not end there. Without their "expression", property relations could not exist at all. Thus the "legal expression" of relations of production, as property, does not merely state that people stand in certain relations, as a fact that is the case whether stated or not, but is requisite for bringing them into those relations.

Hence the language of property, the "legal expression" of the relations of production, without which those relations fall apart and vanish and human association would become unworkable, is of profound importance for the formation of all human relations, of all relations between persons, without exception.

3

Division of Labour and Private Property

The fact that language is requisite to institute property does not mean that it is possible, by saying whatever we please, to institute whatever relations of production we please.

The existence of property means that affairs are regulated by certain prescriptions, that people assume certain rights and obligations. For this it is required, firstly that certain conditions (often quite elaborate ones) must be satisfied without which entitlement to property does not hold good, and secondly that the prescribed rights and obligations must be enforceable. But what prescriptions as to property can be effectively instituted and enforced depends on the circumstances and, above all, on the character of the production process itself. Thus Marx said that people enter into relations of production "independent of their will". How they can and do regulate their social production does not depend on free choice (they do not all get together, as was once imagined, and freely institute a "social contract") but on the character of the social production it is required to regulate.

In their primitive state, possessing only the very crudest and simplest techniques by which they had first raised themselves above other animals, people could live only in small groups, jointly appropriating and sharing out such means of life as they could obtain. They were still completely dependent, like other animals, on the natural conditions of their habitat and what it provided for them. After living in such a condition for countless generations, some people managed to break this dependence by finding out how to cultivate crops and domesticate animals.

The invention of agriculture led to the kinds of human relations with which we are now familiar in recorded history. By breaking their subordination to nature and beginning to subdue nature to human purposes people entered into those relations with each other which led Edward Gibbon to describe history as the record of "the crimes, follies and misfortunes of mankind". Keenly aware of the fact of progress, he yet contrasted the way people actually treated one another with the kind of relations he would have expected were we really, as some have claimed, rational animals—and so queried the value of the progress made and whether anything any better could ever be achieved by man. The same query still demands an answer today. Progress, in the scientific and technological sense, is a fact, but where is it getting us and what is it worth?

Any technique demands some kind of division of labour, with different people performing different functions in the economy. It seems probable that with very primitive techniques the principal division of labour was based on the natural division of the sexes. The invention of agriculture eventually brought new division of labour of a much more artificial and elaborate sort. It led to a greater multiplicity of jobs in growing crops and looking after animals. Then the discovery of the use of metals led to the differentiation of various industrial crafts from agricultural labour. And as population increased and people lived in bigger communities and more contact was established between different communities, it led to the differentiation of both management and distribution from productive labour. All this in turn altered the relations of the sexes and the structure of the family: women became relegated to the dependent and subordinate position which civilised peoples afterwards came to regard as natural. At the same time, labour began to produce a surplus. Whereas in primitive conditions the most that a human group could do by combined productive efforts was to get enough for them all to live on, those engaged in production now produced more than enough for their own subsistence, so that it became possible for non-producers to be supported on the labour of the producers.

The division of labour, with production of a surplus, meant

14

that people entered into new relations of production, which could no longer be expressed in terms of the primitive ideas of communal property with everything being shared out among the members of a group. New forms of property had to be instituted, private property, giving expression to new relations of production within which people could effectively regulate the division of labour which their techniques involved. For as Marx and Engels observed in *The German Ideology* (I, 1) "the various stages of development in the division of labour are just so many different forms of ownership; i.e. the existing stage in the division of labour determines also the relations of individuals to one another with reference to the materials, instruments and products of labour".

Thus instead of everything being shared out, products are exchanged. They pass from hand to hand, and have to be regarded as belonging to the different people who acquire them in the process. Similarly, different means of production came to be regarded as belonging to different individuals or groups of individuals.

Property is a socially regulated form of appropriation. And the most noteworthy feature of private property is that, in acquiring it, people no longer communally appropriate products of communal labour, but individuals or groups within the community appropriate means of production, and articles for use or exchange produced by other individuals or groups. It means that some people acquire an entitlement to the products of other people's labour.

Thus the appropriation of objects as private property, both means of production and means of consumption, consists not simply of a relation between people and objects but of a relation between people and people—a relation of social production.

Private property was not instituted by choice but by necessity, "independent of men's will". Theologians like Aquinas and political philosophers like Locke supposed it natural for men to acquire private property. If that were true, then it would have to be admitted that in civilised communities not only are some people more equal than others but also more natural. It is true, of course, that the human mode of life requires that people should always enter into relations of production, expressed as property relations; but so long as they remained nearest to their natural condition the idea of instituting private property never entered their heads. Private property came into existence out of the (very unnatural) division of labour involved in higher techniques, and it was technological progress which in the first place made it necessary.

Private property was a condition for the technological progress of human communities and for the increase of their command over nature and of their wealth. And it was equally a condition for freeing some people from the drudgery of necessary productive labour and allowing them to develop their intellectual powers, and so for the development and diversification of human interests and human personality, and of culture and the arts. Evidently, it profoundly affected all human relations in a number of ways, making them quite different from the simple and direct person to person relationships characteristic of primitive communities.

Reliable evidence about the historical development of all human communities is, from the nature of the case, rather hard to get, and in many cases not obtainable at all. As Marx's own researches already showed, no simple historical "law" postulating a universal stage-to-stage development for every human community will fit the facts; and while everything people do is conditioned by their social relations of production, not everything they do can be directly attributed to economic causes. In the course of history, as various communities have carried on their social production and adapted their production relations in various ways to their productive forces, diverse formations of property relations (in Marx's phrase, "social-economic formations") have been instituted locally and undergone various metamorphoses. In these, a variety of specific types of human relation arising out of private property have emerged—such as the relation of master and slave, lord

16

and serf, guildmaster and journeyman, capitalist and wage-labourer, and a host of others. But quite apart from such specific relationships established locally, and their effects on all human relations within local communities, it is possible to distinguish certain universal ways in which private property affects human relations, irrespective of the particular form of property.

4

Alienation

The principal and universal effect of division of labour and private property on human relations is to divide people up within communities, in such a way that the labour of some becomes the necessary means which others must subdue to their purposes in òrder to get from it the products they desire.

Hence there is introduced into human relations a man-made asymmetry distinct from the natural asymmetry of the relations of men and women, stronger and weaker, older and younger, parents and children, and so on. This is the asymmetry characteristic of domination and exploitation. It means that people are so divided up and estranged that for some of them other people stand in the relation of depersonalised things or objects, to be used as means to ends, without regard to their personality. It means that what people learn to set a value on is not the enjoyment of human activities but the external objects they can manage to appropriate and to possess which they compete with other people and use other people. This estrangement is superimposed on the natural and personal relationships between human beings, in which all are to each other simply other persons with whom one is living in the community, their differences being simply differences of sex, age, ability, character, and so on. It means that persons or, at all events, their inherent personal capacities exerted when they work, become the property of other persons, to be used up as those others direct—as happens, for example with slaves or serfs or wage-workers. The introduction of man-made asymmetry, or inequality, into human relations means their depersonalisation. The unequal or asymmetrical relations between persons resulting from division of labour and private property are relations holding between them, not by virtue of their being persons with such and such characteristics, but by virtue of their holding or not holding entitlements to property. Hence these relations are not personal ones, which can be voluntarily adjusted as between persons, nor are they simple natural relations, but depersonalised or impersonal relations.

The fact that in the regulated system of production and appropriation some people are treated by others as things, and that, in that respect, they or their personal capacities become other people's property, was described by Marx, in the *Economic and Philosophic Manuscripts*, as "self-alienation", meaning that an integral part of their own persons is alienated as the property of others.

This alienation has a depersonalising effect on human relations generally, and not only on those specific relations in which the alienation occurs. Human fellowship is replaced by relations in which people have to use other people, and to see the end or good of their lives not in relations with other people but in things, and in the use of other people to obtain possession of things. It means that everyone is related to everyone else by impersonal relations, depending on property. Naturally, they are all people and can and do enter into personal relations. But personal relations are conditioned and coloured by impersonal ones. For example, a slaveowner or feudal magnate or employer may be keenly aware of the personalities of slaves, serfs or employees, and do his best to treat them accordingly; and they may even respond with respect and affection. But this does not in the least alter the impersonality of the relationship.

The fact that people are for other people objects for use has fundamentally affected the relations between the sexes. Personal sexual relations based on the natural difference between the sexes, the pleasure and support they naturally afford each other, and the rearing of children, are made unequal in the sense that women are subjected to men and treated as objects—means for sexual use, means for the production of children, and amongst the propertied classes means for alliances of properties, for producing heirs and, very often, as items of property themselves. Thus as well as other divisions a division is created cutting right through the human race, in which the natural difference of sex become a difference of status, and in which the personal relations between the sexes in their sexual activity are partially or even wholly depersonalised.

Such alienation effects in human relations are so well-known from experience as to be perfectly obvious. They have been for so long familiar as to be simply taken for granted, so that few think there is anything remarkable, still less remediable, in human relations being like this.

The introduction of inequality, alienation and depersonalisation into human relations brings into the human community antagonisms entirely distinct from personal antagonisms—oppositions of interest between whole groups or classes of people arising, not from personal disagreements or quarrels, but from differences in their methods of acquisition. These antagonisms are utterly impersonal, and may cut right across the personal likes or dislikes of people for one another; but, willy-nilly, people are caught up in them. The history of all communities thus becomes, as was stated in *The Communist Manifesto*, "the history of class struggles". And because people are for other people things for their use, wars of conquest result and, on the other side, wars of liberation, with all the destruction, cruelty and suffering they bring. The social violence and cruelty which has long been characteristic of human behaviour is not the result of the aggressiveness of human individuals (there is, of course, such an aggressiveness, and it is harnessed in class struggles and wars), but of the property relations into which they have entered in the development of social production.

At the same time the divisions within society have a polarising action, in which the toil is concentrated at one pole and its reward at the other. Thus for the masses of producers (and this has always meant primarily agricultural producers) there is unending toil, filling their whole lives, with a bare subsistence to show for it, and ignorance and squalor without opportunity to enjoy the benefits of the sciences and arts, while the reward of this toil in the way of comfort, luxury, education and culture goes to the opposite pole of society, the ruling class and the privileged. Similarly, the masses are able to exert only manual skills and crafts, while the work of the intellect and of artistic creation is monopolised by a privileged few, dependent on and patronised or employed by the ruling class. And similarly, the advances of civilisation are concentrated in towns, while the rural hinterland remains in backwardness. With every advance in technical accomplishment the effects of this polarising action become greater. The greater the sum of social wealth, the greater becomes the inequality between the wealth of the few and the poverty of the many.

The upshot of alienation and the depersonalisation of human relations is that people in their social activity find themselves subject to impersonal forces—which they themselves have unwittingly created but over which they have no control. Thus human relations themselves confront people as an alien power, influencing their actions and the results of their actions, and determining the relations into which individuals can consciously enter with one another. Hence, unlike production in which men produce what they intend to produce, the development of social relations proceeds in directions independent of and often quite contrary to men's intentions, like any natural process the laws of which are independent of men's will.

In another sense of "alienation", men have collectively alienated their own social relations, and not only that but their own means of production, their own products and their own institutions, so that instead of these being under the collective control of men, subordinated to human purposes, men's lives are subordinate to them. People find themselves passively accepting or struggling to get free of their own alienated creations. Thus in developing the means of production people have become individually subordinate to them, so that the peasant is tied to the land and the animals, and the industrial worker to the machine. The means of production are not the man's servant, but he becomes theirs. When products are produced not for the producers' use but to be appropriated by others and exchanged, men lose collective control over them and instead fall under the control of their own products exercised through the impersonal power of money. In the divided condition of humanity state institutions are set up to maintain social order and direct public policy, and then people become subject to the state. The interests of the state are set up, demanding service and sacrifice from persons in precedence to their personal interests.

5

Religion

The relations into which people enter with one another in obtaining their means of life are reflected in the way they think about human life in general, and human needs. The alienation and depersonalisation of human relations universal in communities that have advanced beyond primitive techniques accounts for religion becoming so pervasive a feature of men's conscious life in such communities.

Religion is the product of this state of human relations. While a number of very primitive ideas and magical practices have been incorporated into religious rituals (for example, scholars have traced Christian rituals back to primitive magic, and Protestant Churches are still reckoned "high" or "low" according to the extent to which their rituals incorporate it), religion is a phenomenon of human consciousness quite distinct from the magic by which primitive peoples try to subdue nature and strengthen their own hands. Religion presupposes a degree of technical progress. It presupposes that the extreme dependence of men upon nature in primitive communities has been overcome, and that therefore the primitive consciousness of union with nature, expressed in magic and animist ideas, has been overcome too. With religion man conceives of himself as a being apart from nature, taking cognisance of the natural properties of things in order to use them for human ends.

There have been and are a variety of religions practised by different people in different circumstances. Moreover, in civilised communities religion is always a two-tier phenomenon. There is religion as understood, obeyed and practised by the uneducated masses, and there is the doctrine and theory adumbrated by officials who direct it from the top. Between these big differences can develop, resulting in mass breakaways.

But ignoring the variegated forms of religion, the contradictions among them and the ways in which they are rationalised in religious doctrines, certain fundamental features remain in common. All religions teach a doctrine of the supernatural, according to which the natural world is a dependency of the supernatural, and man is not a merely natural being but has a stake in the supernatural world. And all religions combine this with teachings about the fallen, lost or sinful condition of man in his natural existence, and about the road to salvation. The combination of conceptions of the supernatural with those of sin and salvation is the hallmark of religion (by itself, a doctrine of the supernatural is merely idealist metaphysics, a by-product of the rationalisation of religion by sophisticated leisure classes).

Evidently, the religious conception of the supernatural presupposes a conception of nature to which the supernatural is opposed. And this presupposes a development of technology which has overcome primitive animist ideas, so that natural processes and their laws are conceived as independent of human activities. Thus, for example, a procedure for turning wine into blood would be, according to primitive conceptions, simply a piece of magic, and not a miraculous abrogation of the laws of nature confirming faith in the supernatural. The religious conception of the miracle contradicts the primitive conception of magic, even though it develops out of it, just as the religious opposition of the supernatural to the natural contradicts primitive animism. Religion introduces into men's ideas of their condition a fundamental dualism—the opposition of man to nature, of the supernatural to the natural, of spirit to matter, and of the eternal and changeless to the temporal and changeable.

This dualism constitutes the ideological essence of religion. Thus religious doctrines are not hypotheses invented to explain the phenomena of nature, which are superseded as the sciences develop other types of hypotheses. Many scientists are still religious: that does not mean that they inconsistently support incompatible hypotheses, since religion is not a hypothesis comparable with those of the sciences. It continues alongside and complementary to the development of technology and natural sciences.

With the conception of the supernatural goes that of sin and salvation. Man, conceived as divided from nature by his spiritual attributes, is conceived as in his natural existence a fallen being. But he can win salvation from this state, though it is not to be realised in this earthly life—and all religious teachings, precepts and rituals are concerned with how to do so. Of course, ideas of what salvation consists of, and of what to do to be saved, vary greatly, as do ideas of the fate of those who remain in sin (though this is always unpleasant). The idea of sin is, along with that of the supernatural, a fundamental idea of all religion, and sin is no more to be described in empirical terms than is the supernatural. Thus to say that people are sinful is not the same as to describe typical modes of behaviour and express disapproval. Sin does not consist merely of bad behaviour (though, as Saint Paul made clear, the sinful nature of men results in their bad behaviour). Nor does salvation from sin consist of finding the way to lead a good and happy life on earth.

Religion has been condemned on the grounds that it is a system of illusions propagated by agents of the ruling classes to deceive the masses. Yet it did not arise by being imposed on the masses, but arose from amidst the masses themselves. It has been condemned for serving to support systems of exploitation and to incite to and justify man's inhumanity to man. Yet both oppression and the fight against it, cruelties and the protest against them, individual greed and the ways of altruism and self-sacrifice, savage wars and persecutions and appeals for tolerance and reconciliation have been practised in the name of religion and been apparently inspired by religious ideas and motives. The fact is that religion is not simply a system of doctrines craftily worked out, and it is not itself a primary motive power in society, either for good or ill. It is the reflection in ideas of the alienated human relations within which all men's social action takes place.

The lives of men, the realisation of their intentions, and their relations with each other, are dominated by an impersonal power which has no natural origin or explanation. In the human community man is opposed to man, actuated by something inherent in but alien to himself. These are the objective circumstances reflected in religion—in the religious ideas of supernatural power, and of the lost and sinful condition of men from which we can escape only by seeking a salvation not of this world. These fundamental and universal religious ideas are thus the reflection in human consciousness of the alienation of human relations. The language of religion is the peculiar and universal language in which people come to represent to themselves their condition and their relations with each other and with nature, when they have still found no way of comprehending how they have brought themselves into this condition, or of bringing what they have alienated under their own conscious purposive control.

The universal prevalence of religion is due to the universal occurrence of conditions in which men lack control over the social use of their own means of satisfying their needs. According to religion, men can never satisfy their needs without help—and that help is not the mundane help of other men, nor the help afforded by scientific knowledge, but extra-human supernatural help. In the dualistic religious conception of man and his needs, the nature of man is divided into the material and the spiritual, and his spiritual needs are offset against his material ones. The sorrows of the material deprivation of the masses and the divided condition of mankind are compensated by the spiritual consolations of religion.

Hence, as Marx was already insisting in his *Contribution to the Critique of Hegel's Philosophy of Law* (1843), the criticism of religion is the criticism of the human conditions which give rise to religion, and the criticism of the religious conception of the human condition and of human needs must rest upon the investigation of the actual condition and needs of men, and of how men by their own efforts can satisfy their needs. The people cannot find the way to "their real happiness" so long as they seek "the illusory happiness" provided in religion.

"The demand to give up illusions about their condition is the demand to give up a condition that requires illusions. . . . The immediate task of philosophy, which is at the service of history, once the other-worldly form of human self-alienation has been unmasked, is to unmask self-alienation in its this-worldly form. Thus the criticism of heaven turns into the criticism of the earth, the criticism of religion into the criticism of rights, and the criticism of theology into the criticism of politics."

6

Capitalism and Socialism

Capitalist property and capitalist production relations, which have been instituted in modern times, represented the extreme limit, and so the final form, of the process described by Marx as human "self-alienation".

With capitalism all products are produced as commodities, and labour-power and, indeed, all human abilities are put up for sale and so alienated by their possessors. The depersonalisation of human relations reaches an extreme in which the subordination of some people to others takes the form of the subordination of them all to completely impersonal organisations. Thus in a feudal society, for example, men were subject to their lord or their king; but in a capitalist society, while some give orders for others to carry out, the employee is equal as a person to his boss and the employer is a corporation—of a peculiar type instituted by monetary statements of entitlement to property. The holdings of capitalist corporations are derived from appropriations of the products of labour, so that, as Marx put it, their sway represents the rule of "dead" over "living" labour. The great capitalist monopolies and trusts, and the capitalist machinery of state, are faceless and impersonal. Of course, a capitalist community, like any other, is nothing but a lot of people doing things together and speaking to each other; but their relations to each other, and how they treat each other, are governed by impersonal profit-making and profit-disposing organisations, and every relationship in which people live and work together is governed by considerations about money, by the impersonal and alien power of money which has the last say in what they can or cannot do together. Personal deprivation takes new forms. Even as extremes of deprivation of material goods become alleviated, people are increasingly turned loose and left to fend for themselves in their personal lives. The individualistic protest which increases under capitalism, and takes all manner of unconventional and on occasion anti-social forms, is the response to this.

At the same time, the polarisation in society continues, acting not only inside each capitalist community but on a world scale. Men are increasingly equalised, as personal privileges of birth and rank disppear. But the more democratisation and equalisation there is, the more marked becomes the division of classes and the more dangerous and intractable become the conflicts on a world scale. The so-called "disappearance of class distinctions" in capitalist democracies, and the formal recognition that all people are equal members of the human race, only serve to reveal in their nakedness the class conflicts and national conflicts as based on nothing but impersonal divisions of interest. And these conflicts are then revealed as human anomalies, due only to the degree of subjection of persons to an impersonal system.

But if capitalism is the extreme of the alienation process in human relations, it also brings into being the conditions to end it.

Capitalist relations are instituted when the development of relatively advanced techniques demands the purchase of labour-power for the purpose of employing a number of people to work together in a single enterprise. And once the capitalist relations are in operation, the drive for profits from which to accumulate more capital, together with the competition of different capitals, leads to the continuous improvement of techniques. The search begins for motive powers other than those of animals and human muscle (water power, steam power, the internal combustion engine, electrical energy, nuclear power), and the development of mass production methods powered by them. Under capitalism there occurs not only a revolution in techniques but, as *The Communist Manifesto* put it, a continuous revolutionising of techniques. Scientific research is developed as itself a new force of production. The sciences do not simply investigate nature but, by their discoveries, change the relationship of man and nature, by equipping men with new powers.

As a result, a stage has been reached when techniques are available completely to satisfy the material needs of the whole human race. The means and knowhow actually exist to provide abundance to a large population, and to do so with a minimum expenditure of muscular energy, without arduous labour or a high proportion of individuals' time being demanded by labour, so that plenty of leisure, with opportunities for education and enjoyment, should be the right of everyone. Despite the existing mass poverty and technological backwardness throughout large areas, and facing up to and overcoming problems of pollution and of control of population, the realisation of such a state of affairs could now be technically accomplished. The obstacle is not lack of means but the human relations which prevent people from uniting to deploy the means.

When men have changed their relationship with nature they can also change their relations with each other. As was enunciated in Marx's fundamental proposition about social development, a change in the first always necessitates a change in the second.

The technological development under capitalism changes the character of the labour process and of the division of labour. This change can be expressed in one word by saying that production becomes socialised. Instead of the production of the totality of goods needed by a community being done by a large number of separate individuals and groups, each working independently and each contributing one product which they themselves or others must appropriate, production is more and more concentrated within large-scale enterprises. A large number of people work together according to a production-plan to produce their output jointly or socially.

Although the development of modern technology began by accentuating the earlier effects of division of labour on human personality, by tying individuals to particular parts of the processes of mass production and making them the servants of machines, its long-term demand is for highly educated people with a grasp of the production process as a whole. The use of modern technology demands individuals who are not the servants but the makers and masters of machines, and for whom, moreover, labour is not the dominant factor in their individual lives. This was already stressed by Marx (in *Capital*), but the most recent developments of automation underline it even more. By the development of technology capitalism set in motion a new development of the division of labour, reversing the old. This is in contradiction to the division of the community into the rulers and the ruled, the educated thinking elite and the ignorant uneducable mass, which nevertheless it is the whole tendency of the property relations to retain.

The socialisation of production under capitalism, then, brings into existence conditions in which it is possible to put an end to relations in which the capacities of some are treated as the property of others, with all the effects which ensue from that. But not only is this possible, it is necessary, if the processes of production are not to be continually interrupted by human conflicts and economic breakdown.

The system of private appropriation, which originally developed out of the division of labour, and which survives in capitalist property relations, is no longer in accord with the new socialised form of production. As Engels put it in *Socialism, Utopian and Scientific*, socialised production is "subjected to a form of appropriation which presupposes the private production of individuals . . . The mode of production is subjected to this form of appropriation, although it abolishes the conditions upon which the latter rests." Consequently there exists a contradiction between "socialised production and capitalist appropriation" and "between the organisation of production in the individual workshop and the anarchy of production in society generally . . . The mode of production is in rebellion against the mode of exchange." Socialised production requires to be socially planned in accordance with social resources and needs, and to be matched by social appropriation, in which entitlement to products rests simply on being a person, a member of society, and not on the ownership of property.

Capitalist private property can and must be converted into social property. How can this come about? Unhappily, with

31

the human race divided and estranged from each other as they are, it cannot possibly come about by general agreement. It can only come about, as other revolutionary changes in property relations have done, through class struggle. Wherever class conflicts exist they cannot but be fought to a conclusion, however long it takes and however much some may wish to bring about a reconciliation.

The socialisation of production in the countries of advanced technology accentuates the contradiction of interest between the magnates of capital and the working people of their own and of the underdeveloped countries. And the result is, as *The Communist Manifesto* showed, that by organising and hastening the development of socialised production "what the bourgeoisie produces, above all, are its own gravediggers". The effect is to bring together and organise in opposition to capital whole populations of working people.

The difference between this conflict and earlier ones between exploited and exploiting classes is that, with the new character of production, the exploited become organised and educated. There is no further need for a privileged class of rulers, to manage public affairs; the working people themselves have become quite capable of providing the personnel for that purpose.

The original cause of the estrangement within human communities was division of labour leading to private property. And property is the issue of every irreconcilable conflict between men. Property relations are not unchangeable. They are instituted by men and can be changed by men. But the reconstitution of property comes about, and this is the only way it can come about, as the outcome of class struggle. The power to preserve property relations or to change them is the power to make and to enforce laws. Consequently the final issue of the struggle against capital is the issue of securing this power. The practical conclusion of Marx about the struggle for socialism was that it is and can only be a political struggle, based on and mobilising the forces of the classes opposed to capital, with the object of obtaining political or state power to institute a radical change in property relations.

7

Communism

In his Preface to the English edition (1888) of *The Communist Manifesto*, Engels thus summed up the conclusion of Marxist social theory: "The history of class struggles forms a series of evolutions in which, nowadays, a stage has been reached where the exploited and oppressed class cannot attain its emancipation from the sway of the exploiting and ruling class without, at the same time, and once and for all, emancipating society at large from all exploitation, oppression, class distinction and class struggles."

The fundamental law of development of human society discovered by Marx—the law that men must always bring their relations of production into accordance with their forces of production—does not (as I have already remarked) state any preordained sequence of stages of social development through which every human community must inevitably pass. On the contrary, new forces of production are only developed in rather exceptional local circumstances, and many communities have set up social relations incapable of development, in which they have remained stuck until overrun and overcome by the aggression of others. But Marx's discovery leads to three conclusions about the overall course of social development. It may be noted that these conclusions are not statements of what is deterministically inevitable, but take the form proper to scientific conclusions—that is, they delimit possibilities.

To begin with, the development of forces of production could only take place under conditions of private appropriation, the exploitation of labour, the alienation of human capacities and the depersonalisation of human relations, divided communities and class struggles.

In these circumstances, the sequence of technological progress was bound up with the production of products as commodities. The eventual outcome, bound by the working out of probabilities to be arrived at somewhere some time, whatever digressions and deadends particular communities might get into, could only be the formation of capitalist property relations and the socialisation of production.

Now that outcome has been reached, the sequence of class struggles can be brought to an end with the assumption of power by the exploited class and the institution of socialist relations of production.

"The bourgeois relations of production," wrote Marx in the Preface to *The Critique of Political Economy*, "are the last antagonistic form of the social process of production . . . at the same time the productive forces developing in the womb of bourgeois society create the material conditions for the solution of that antagonism. This social formation brings, therefore, the pre-history of human society to a close."

Once power has passed from the hands of the classes whose mode of appropriation is based on private property, it is possible to begin to transform property relations by making the means and products of socialised production public or co-operative property. This begins the reconstitution of the relations of men to men corresponding to the establishment of the new relationship of men to nature in socialised production. It stops the labour-power of some being the property of others, and by ending capitalist appropriation abolishes the exploitation of man by man and the conflicts forced on men by the impersonal antagonistic relations of classes.

On this basis it is possible to plan social production so as steadily to increase the quantity and improve the quality of the goods and services available to each individual. And at the same time, with the scientific development of technology, it is possible progressively to shorten the necessary working day for each individual, and to ensure that the necessity of working, imposed on men by their relationship with nature, becomes a pleasure instead of a burden. It is possible, as Marx claimed (*Capital*, III, 48, 3), that men should carry out the task of necessary work "with the least expenditure of energy and under conditions most favourable to and worthy of their human nature", and that it should serve them as the basis for free personal activity and personal relations—"that development of human energy which is an end in itself".

The basis is then established for conceptions of men and their needs radically different from the prevailing religious ones. Human needs are now understood as arising solely from the human mode of life rooted in social production, and capable of satisfaction through men's efforts alone. Men are not divided into a degraded material and a higher spiritual part, and need no supernatural help or guidance. Yet their needs are not confined to material needs, in the sense of requirements for the biological functioning of human bodies and the continuation of the species. The characteristic human need is for personal relations with other people. People need human companionship, sympathy, assistance and co-operation first of all to produce together the material means of life and then, on that basis, to develop and enjoy the activities and fruits of human culture. While none of this is possible unless elementary material needs are satisfied (so that to preach that material satisfactions are worthless in comparison with "spiritual" ones is utterly repugnant to the development of human relations and human personality), the material needs of men are themselves humanised and transformed into specifically human as distinct from animal needs. Thus people do not simply need food but need it artfully prepared and served, they do not simply need clothing and shelter but fashions and architecture, and they do not simply need sexual intercourse but the art of love and human relations between the sexes. Communism is not a new religion, but makes all religion pointless. It establishes the conditions in which people can begin purposively to co-operate to make possible for all the satisfaction of their needs.

The first tasks of socialist revolution are political—to change the state from an organisation functioning to protect private appropriation into one functioning to prevent it; to expand the state by instituting organisation for managing socialist production; and to protect socialist property and put down any efforts to subvert it. These are the tasks covered in Marx's famous phrase "the dictatorship of the proletariat".

These political tasks combine with economic ones—to plan production and distribution so as to deploy all available resources, materials, machinery and labour, to produce the goods and services people need and to share them out; and to expand scientific research and education so as to develop the techniques of planned production, lighten labour and make more and better goods and services available.

The goal of socialist politics and socialist planning is, obviously, to produce an absolute abundance of goods and services, so that all that anyone can need is available to him. And, apart from obstacles of external interference, natural calamities and errors of planning, all of which are surmountable, there is no reason why this goal should not be reached.

The eventual and final abolition of shortages constitutes the economic condition for entering upon a communist society. When there is socialised production the products of which are socially appropriated, when science and scientific planning have resulted in the production of absolute abundance, and when labour has been so lightened and organised that all can without sacrifice of personal inclinations contribute their working abilities to the common fund, everyone will receive a share according to his needs. This economic principle of communism was that propounded by the English philosopher William Godwin: "From each according to his ability, to each according to his need."

Before communism can come into operation, however, the affairs of socialist society (called by Marx "the first phase of communism", or the "transitional" phrase from capitalism to communism) have to be managed on a different principle: "From each according to his ability, to each according to his work."

Evidently, the socialisation of property in means of production does no more than initiate a change in human relations. It makes it possible of completion, but does not complete it.

Socialism abolishes the primary condition of self-alienation, in that no person's abilities are any longer appropriated for the use of another person. But in the socialist economy goods and services are still allocated to each person "according to his work", which means, as Marx put it in *The Critique of the Gotha Programme*, the continuation of unequal "bourgeois right". Defects, he said, "are inevitable in the first phase of communist society, as it is when it has just emerged after prolonged birth pangs from capitalist society. Right can never be higher than the economic structure of society and its cultural development conditioned thereby." Once a socialist economy is well established (as it is today, for example, in the U.S.S.R.) all exploitation of man by man is indeed abolished. All are working together now for the benefit of each. Yet some of the effects of the earlier condition of alienation remain—the inequalities of persons (as Marx put it, their "unequal rights for unequal labour"), the depersonalisation of human relations and subjection of persons to impersonal organisations. What each person can offer by way of labour is still appropriated by a public organisation, and his entitlement to recompense depends on the value it places on what it gets from him. People are still related to each other through their individual relations to an impersonal organisation. They have created this organisation for their own benefit, to an increasing extent they democratically control it, but they still make themselves subject to it. And how they can each develop and help or hinder each other depends not alone on each of them personally but on what they have set up over themselves. With socialism, therefore, for a time at least, some of the alienation effects experienced under capitalism may even be accentuated. For the power and scope of impersonal organisation, and its control over and direction of what people do, increases.—This is a point important to understand, for otherwise we may be surprised and dismayed at the deplorable things that can still happen in socialist society, which we had hoped could never happen there.

But socialist economic development itself removes the causes of these alienation effects and paves the way for men being finally able to get rid of them in communist society.

Having been depersonalised, human relations can be personalised. Having been made indirect and impersonal, they can be made direct and personal. The relations of millions of people, most of whom can never meet, can be made as personal as those of a group of friends, because they are all engaged together in the common enterprise and adventure of human life. Then, as Marx said (*Capital*, I, 1, 4), "the practical relations of everyday life offer to man none but perfectly intelligible and reasonable relations with regard to his fellow men and to nature".

This ending of the depersonalisation of human relations, and making relations between persons personal, "perfectly intelligible and reasonable", involves two main changes.

The division of society into antagonistic classes made necessary the setting up of states, with their apparatus of law-making and enforcement, of administration and coercion, a public power exercised by people but standing over them to make and enforce public policies to ensure that some interests prevail over others. In the first place, therefore, the ending of class divisions and the impersonal conflicts between classes makes this public power a human anomaly. Special organisations to govern people, with armies, police and officials, together with all the political organisations and parties which have been formed with the object of creating a power to influence and direct state power, will no longer be needed and so can be disbanded. The state, as Engels expressed it, can be made to "wither away". For "state interference in social relations becomes, in one domain after another, superfluous, and then dies out of itself; the government of persons is replaced by the administration of things, and by the conduct of processes of production" (*Socialism, Utopian and Scientific*, 3).

In the second place, the organisation of production itself changes. In socialism, the state takes charge of production. The means of production become state-property. And as class antagonisms disappear in a socialist society, the state ceases to have any function of class repression but continues to function as owner and manager (and protector) of public property. There thus exists an organisation which employs people and makes available to them goods and services in accordance with their work. But eventually the conduct of processes of production can be arranged by people simply working together to make use of things to satisfy their needs, instead of being governed by an organisation standing over them and making use of them for the purpose of publicly appropriating and distributing things.

In socialist society the production plan still takes the form of "law", an act of state, made and enforced by a planning authority. However much democratic consultation goes on, the planners are still the agents of an impersonal authority—an authority for the government of persons as well as for the administration of things. As resources increase and techniques become more powerful, the problems to be solved in a plan become more complex; and, so it would seem, the more necessary becomes the role of a competent planning authority as a organ of government. But this very complexity of the problems also means that no human agency could possibly solve them without mechanical aid, any more than it could move mountains. The advance of techniques includes techniques of data-processing, communication, computing and directing the use of techniques—and would grind to a stop unless these were included. Hence rather than depending entirely on the brain-power of a planning authority, consisting of technocrats who work out what is to be done and give orders accordingly, planning must itself become automated. People will use automata to plan production and distribution, just as they use machines to make things and transport them. The most complete automation of the action of persons on things in social production is the condition for the most complete humanisation of the relations of persons with persons.

Such a change in human relations means, essentially, that individual personality is no longer subordinated either to the acquisitive use of other persons or to the service and direction of impersonal organisations and powers. There are only the direct and intelligible personal relations of living individuals, each of whom depends on others for the development of his own personality, as well as for the benefit of the techniques which they all employ together for getting their requirements from nature and making them available to each other.

Communism does not, of course, mean anything so unlikely as that no one will ever quarrel or disagree with anyone else, or deceive or injure anyone else, or ever be discontented, or that all will be equally wise and high-minded, and human stupidity never again bring human enterprise to grief. It does mean that social injustice, oppression and strife, the insolence of office and the ostentation of wealth, will be ended along with cultural deprivation and material want. When techniques have been developed to the point when the whole of social production and distribution can be rationally planned for the satisfaction of the needs of all, society can become simply an association of equal persons with no other end than to serve the interests of each individual as an end in himself. The interests of no privileged person or group, and no social organisation, can then claim precedence over the individual needs of any single person. Then, as Marx put it, the "pre-history" of human society will have been brought to a close. And instead of social events being explicable only in terms of relations into which people enter independent of their will, of impersonal conflicts in which they find themselves involved and have to fight out, and of consequences of their actions which no one intended, they will be explained in terms of how people judged, chose and decided.

8

Science and Evaluation

The demonstration of what it is possible to make of human life by progress to communism is at the same time a demonstration of its desirability. It establishes *factual* judgments about the actual character and mode of development of forces of production and relations of production; practical or *political* judgments about what has to be done and who has to do it, if human relations are to be developed in conformity with the possibilities and requirements of technological progress; and, finally, *value* judgments about the desirability of the end and the merit of the struggle to reach it.

The scientific ideas of communism about social development and human personality, and likewise its ideas about how to conduct the politics of class struggle, are not derived from moral concepts or value judgments; they are derived from investigation of human relations and experience of class struggle. On the other hand, moral concepts and value judgments are derived from the scientific and political ideas of communism. Thus communism is not founded on principles of morality but, on the other hand, it enunciates foundations for value judgments. Communism does not by a moral argument deduce an ideal of human association and standards of conduct but, on the other hand, by examining the actual conditions and possibilities of human association and the causes and effects of different kinds of conduct it finds the reasons for judging one form of association more desirable than another, and one mode of conduct better than another.

At the same time, the value judgments which the scientific ideas of communism lead to are not in contradiction to those which have been previously evolved during the progressive development of mankind. Communism does not contradict the traditional conceptions of human values exemplified in the condemnation of greed, cruelty and oppression, the assertion of the rights of individuals, the inviolability of human personality and the brotherhood of men; on the contrary, it embraces them, justifies them by sufficient reasons and shows the way to convert them from ideals into realities.

The evaluative significance of the scientific ideas of communism was already shown very clearly in the work of Marx.

Marx's arguments for replacing capitalism by socialism are not "moral" arguments, in the commonly accepted sense. Yet they are arguments in favour of doing something, in support of certain prescriptive judgments of value. Marx did not simply make a prediction: capitalism will in fact be replaced by socialism, because the laws of social development make it inevitable. He did not merely advise people to make a virtue of necessity by voluntarily acting in the way they were compelled by the laws of history to act anyhow. He investigated the actual development of relations of production, and on this he based prescriptive practical judgments to guide action to change them in a desirable way. He never supposed socialism would be brought into being without the prescribed collective action, or that it could not fail. He stated facts; but he did not merely state facts, in stating them he execrated them and, on the other hand, warmly advocated the new conditions that should replace them. And the more clearly, fully and factually he described the existing conditions and what should replace them, the greater was the moral force with which he drove home his condemnation of the one and advocacy of the other.

This mixed descriptive-evaluative character of Marx's social analysis has been remarked on by a number of his readers. Professor Popper drew attention to it in the second volume of *The Open Society and its Enemies*. Again, Professor E. J. Hobsbawm remarks in his Introduction to the English translation of Marx's *Pre-capitalist Economic Formations* that Marx's theory is "a model of facts, but, seen from a slightly different angle, the *same* model provides us with value-judgments".

With the development of the sciences in modern times it has

become an axiom in some quarters that questions of fact, such as are ascertained by the sciences, are logically unconnected with questions of value. If you are making a scientific inquiry you are unconcerned with questions about values, and if you are engaged in making evaluations you are not engaged in any kind of scientific enquiry. The confusion of both thought and action leading to and resulting from this antithesis is extreme. There is confusion about science and also confusion about values; but the root of it is confusion about science.

Of course, the conclusions of science must not be influenced by antecedent valuations, in the sense that a scientific inquiry must always test its conclusions in terms of what is the case and not of what someone thinks ought to be the case. But that does not mean that scientific generalisation, on the one hand, and evaluation on the other, are separate and independent matters.

The setting of them in antithesis results in the first place from taking natural sciences as the model, and ignoring the special character of social science. When a physicist generalises about the behaviour of atoms, his conclusions merely show how atoms in fact behave and have no bearing on how they ought to behave. This is not surprising, since such words as "ought" apply only in prescribing the behaviour of people and have no meaning if applied to atoms. But social science differs from natural science in that it deals with people. And generalisations about people, stating the actual conditions of their lives and effects of their actions, do have some bearing on deciding what people ought to do.

In the second place, the antithesis results from so limiting the scope of social science that it is not permitted to generalise in the way natural sciences do. In accordance with the old positivist philosophy of science, social science is limited to stating particular facts and formulating statistical correlations. Of course, if scientific inquiry is so limited, social science remains on a merely classificatory and descriptive level, and is not permitted to arrive at the sort of generalisation familiar in the natural sciences and which, in social science, does become relevant to the foundation of evaluations. Such generalisations do not merely describe social relations, but show how people can and do change them corresponding to the development of their actual means of satisfying their needs, and therefore how both existing relations and men's aspirations and aims to change them satisfy or fall short of human needs and possibilities of developing human capacities.

If, indeed, we are ever to find good reasons for judgments about what is socially desirable, this requires first of all an accurate description of the current state of society—its economic basis, the interests and conflicts of interest contained within it, the individual and collective needs which people have acquired in it and the ways in which and extent to which the current social relations permit their satisfaction, and the possibilities of maintaining social stability or of effecting social changes. And it requires, secondly, a scientifically based general theory about man and his social life. It is such a theory that provides the basis of evaluations, for standards of judgment. For it permits a comparison of the actual with the possible which provides insight into the defects of our social relations and modes of social behaviour relative to the objective requirements for the development of social life, and into practical ways of overcoming them. In other words, if only we can work out a scientifically based general theory of man and society, we can do what so many would-be scientific moralists and philosophers say is logically impossible, namely, find a way both practical and rational of concluding from what the human situation is to what ought to be done in it, and of finding reasons for what we think ought to be done in the investigation of the human situation.

The chief reason why it has been argued that value judgments can never be based on science is that those who argue like this refuse to admit that social investigation can do any more than record lists of facts—they deny it the right enjoyed by other branches of science to establish a general theory. In actual practice, however, people always do argue from an account of a particular set-up, judged in the light of a general theory (however vague and implicit that general theory may be), to the conclusion that certain things are desirable or undesirable, and ought to be changed or left alone. And those who disagree, argue by denying that the current set-up is as described, or denying the general theory, or denying both. For example, I have yet to meet anyone who admitted the truth of Marxist general theory and of its particular descriptive analysis of capitalism, and at the same time denied the Marxist conclusion of the desirability of replacing capitalism by socialism; they have always found fault with some item of the general theory or of the particular analysis or both.

On questions of social desirability, reasoned judgment is always based, and cannot but be based, on theories about the actual conditions of human existence. And likewise when it comes to questions of the rights and wrongs of individual conduct and personal relations, no reasons can be given for what is right and what is wrong without presupposing some such theory. Such theories have traditionally been religious—and hence the widespread idea that morality is inseparable from religion. But there are also all manner of non-religious or lay theories. The real point for moral reasoning must be, first of all, to discuss and test such theories, and then to test value judgments in the light of the theories and in the course of practical experience.

The claim of Marxism is precisely to have established the foundations of a general scientific theory of man and society, of the conditions of human existence. And so it is that the generalisations which Marx established for social science, comparable with those established as the foundations of other departments of science, provide a basis, and a truly scientific basis, for evaluations.

This means that not only does the Marxist scientific approach to social questions formulate aims for the present, but the same generalisations on which present aims are based are the basis for evaluation of the past. The Marxist historical approach not only tries to explain what happened, but the way it explains it is the basis for evaluating it, for evaluating historical actions, institutions and movements and, in another sense, social, political and moral ideas. Such evaluation is, indeed, inseparable from the scientific approach to history. If the study of history is regarded as nothing but making a record of events, then naturally it is not evaluative—but neither is it scientific. So far from the scientific approach to society and its history being antithetical to evaluation, the approach which fails to evaluate fails as science.

Scientific generalisation about people and society shows that people can live only by co-operating to obtain their requirements from nature, that they depend on each other, and that they can develop their human nature and human powers only by adapting relations of production to forces of production. Consequently, it shows the deprivations they suffer, in relation to human needs and the latent possibilities of human life, while they remain in primitive conditions and while they suffer the effects of self-alienation.

It is only in our present epoch, when, as Marx put it, social relations have developed to the stage which "brings the pre-history of human society to a close", that it is at length possible for these deprivations to be overcome. And it is now, when to end alienation effects has become a practical question in the field of social action, that the corresponding science can be and is worked out in the field of social theory. Science then establishes the sufficient reasons for the practical desirability of the communist reconstitution of human relations, and of everything that can tend to overcome, and can finally remove, the alienation effects in human relations. This value judgment is not founded merely on the sentiments of approbation or pleasure which may be evoked by the image of personal relations free from impersonal conflicts, and of everyone having the opportunity to satisfy his needs—though there does go with it the cultivation of such sentiments. It is founded on the scientific demonstration that this is what people can and must do in order to develop the mode of human co-operation by which they live.

The guiding principle of the scientific materialist communist humanist method of arriving at value judgments is that what is worth while, what is good, what is right, what ought to be aimed at and done in human relations and human behaviour is what promotes the human mode of existence—or, as Marx put it in the *Economic and Philosophic Manuscripts*, "realises the human essence". It is what promotes that mode of existence in which people co-operate to obtain what they require, and in which the development of the personality of each is aided by and aids that of others.

This principle establishes, in terms of human relations, the objective standard by reference to which value judgments can be based, not on individual and subjective sentiments and aspirations, or, for that matter, on class interests, but on sufficient reasons.

For ages and ages the common people, and the representatives of progressive thought, have proclaimed these human values and deplored and condemned whatever goes counter to them, even while they have accepted the class values and moral codes thrown up by particular social formations. But they have proclaimed them as aspirations hardly realisable, or as realisable only by individuals or sects who separate themselves from the mass of sinful humanity; as drawn down as revelations from heaven, not as rooted in the earthly existence of men. What Marxist social theory does is to discover the foundations for human values—the reasons for them, the demonstration of their universalisability or objectivity—in the science of man; and at the same time discover how men, when they have advanced to the stage where they are able to establish the science of man, can conduct and win a struggle to make the conditions for a good life not a dream but an everyday reality. It strips the idea of a good life of its supernatural glamour, as something to be earned by the happy elect in another world, and presents it in commonplace terms as descriptive of ordinary people going about their worldly business.

9

Human Values and Class Interests

The primary moral questions, on which the answers to others depend, concern the desirability of forms of human association.

The Marxist approach is to find a reasoned answer to such questions by examining the actual way in which human society, on which all individuals depend, is and has to be kept going. It finds the standard of objective value judgment in the fact that people associate to produce their means of life, and that their form of association either helps or hinders the development and social use of their forces of production. The communist aim is for the establishment of those personal relations between people, free of earlier self-alienation and impersonal restraints and conflicts, in which they can develop and use all the resources of technology for the satisfaction of human needs and, on that basis, freely enjoy as individuals "that development of human energy which is an end in itself". Thus Communism does what all humanist philosophies have sought to do—validate value judgments by reference to the conditions of existence of men as men. It does this, however, not by appealing to sentiments and desires, inclinations allegedly inherent in each separate individual, but by ascertaining the necessary conditions of association for utilising those forces of production by which alone people support their social life and create and satisfy their needs.

In the current circumstances of division of class interests, the communist aim corresponds to some class interests in opposition to others, and demands the subordination of the latter to the former and, eventually, their complete elimination. Aims which do not accord with interests cannot be practicable aims—and therefore there is no sense in arguing about their desirability, since desirability entails practicability. Aims only become real aims and desirable aims when they express

48

interests: they are not, as Marx and Engels insisted in *The German Ideology*, conjured up out of some abstract philosophical conception of man and his good, but they are practically conceived and find expression in the actual historical struggles of living people. But yet the reasoning which validates value judgments does not validate the communist aim merely because it accords with particular interests, but rather values those interests and asserts their over-riding claim, because the interests of working people are ever bound up with the development of human co-operation to satisfy human needs (the human way of life), which can at last be practically realised in the communist aim of the modern working-class movement. As Marx and Engels said, the aim of socialism and communism only emerged from the realm of utopia and became a practical aim with the formation of the modern industrial working class, and only the conscious struggle of that class against those whose interests are opposed to it can bring socialism and communism into being. But the reason for the desirability of the social aim, and for the subordination of some interests to others which it entails until such time as it is completely achieved, is not concerned with the particular interests of particular persons or classes but with what has to be done to bring about relations of production within which people can continue to develop the use of the forces of production they have already created. For to bring relations of production into line with forces of production is what people have to do, what men as men have to do, to carry on their human mode of life. As things are, such a requisite change in relations of production is in the interests of some people (the great majority who do the productive work) and not of others. Hence it involves social conflicts based on conflicts of class interests, and the requirement, rooted in the way human life has actually developed, of subordinating some interests to others.

An argument from class interests, which merely says "We are workers and socialism is in the interests of the working class, therefore our moral duty is to aim at socialism", has some force as an incentive to struggle, but none at all as establishing value judgments. And like much bad logic, it is also in the long run ineffective in practice. It has nothing to say to workers who feel that their personal interests might suffer in the course of any big social change, and who do not see why they should make personal sacrifices for a cause. It has nothing to say to middle-class people and intellectuals. And, since class interest is considered the source of obligation, it implies that while workers rightfully strive for socialism, capitalists just as rightfully strive to stop them getting it. In fact, capitalists do so; but a socialist argument which implies that it is right and just for them to do so is inconsistent and unconvincing. It is proper that in conducting a struggle for socialism which mainly depends on mass working-class economic and political struggle, the appeal should continually be made to the defence and promotion of working-class interests. But in practice much *more* is required than appeals to class interests, and much more is always said in socialist argument. The appeal is always made to conceptions of "humanity"—to the idea that personal or sectional interests ought to be subordinated to the common good, and that socialism is desirable for the sake not merely of the interests of the working class but of the future of humanity. Capitalists pursuing their own profit stand condemned from the human point of view. And workers fighting for their emancipation as a class are justified. What is involved in class struggles is *more* than a clash of interests.

As Engels showed, today the emancipation of the exploited class means "emancipating society at large from all exploitation, oppression, class distinction and class struggles". That is why Lenin, in his address to the Communist youth on *The Tasks of the Youth Leagues* (1920), after saying "Our morality is derived from the interests of the class struggle of the proletariat . . . communist morality is the morality which serves this struggle, which unites the toilers against exploitation...", went on to say: "Morality serves the purpose of helping human society to rise to a higher level and to get rid of the exploitation of labour. . . . The basis of communist morality is the struggle for the consolidation and completion of communism."

10

Ends and Means

All considerations of human values—of what is right or just or good or desirable, and of what ought or ought not to be done, and what is praiseworthy and what is blameworthy—involve considerations about ends and means, and the subordination of means to ends. Broadly speaking, in rational moral judgment the end justifies the means. And not only is this true but in practice this truth is almost universally recognised. For example, a war is thought just if it is waged for just ends. The important questions that have to be answered concern the validation of human ends, and what means they exact.

Rational value judgment about ends and means is not at all the same thing as machiavellian calculation. So-called machiavellianism consists of exclusive preoccupation with particular *interests* (or, as often happens, with what are mistakenly imagined to be those interests), and of saying that anything may be done that serves them. Thus, for example, the machiavellian Prince was advised to practise any cruelty or dirty trick that he could get away with, so long as it enhanced his power. Similarly, it might be said, from a machiavellian point of view, that any standards of good faith or humanity are quite irrelevant to the pursuit of working-class interests, as they are to that of capitalist interests. Keep faith with no one, if advantage is to be got by breaking it. Kill, oppress and torture whenever there is terror to be spread and advantage to be gained by it. The relevant question here concerns what sort of society would actually be built, and what sort of ends attained, if people acted only on such principles.

In practice, the machiavellian point of view is never adopted by masses but cases have occurred where it is adopted by leaders. Such leaders generally see interests only in the form of power, so that what preoccupies them is the preservation and enlargement of their own power. While they get put into power as representatives of a class, their career often ends by the class having to get rid of them.

The divorce which some have made between political questions on the one hand, and moral ones on the other, is totally alien and contradictory to the scientific socialist conception of human ends. This kind of separation, indeed, has no place in socialist political theory, but was made in the political theory of exploiting classes. And wherever it has intruded into political practice, the results have shown that it hinders rather than helps the realisation of socialist and communist aims. The practice of cold political calculation, which regards persons as mere means to be used for political ends, not only repels many who might otherwise be won for socialism, but also disorientates and disorganises the socialist movement itself—quite apart from the fact that such calculations are usually erroneous anyway, since they forget to take into account important human factors.

For scientific socialism and communism, politics is a means and not an end, and moreover a means which, as Marx and Engels stressed in their theory of the state, should be discarded as soon as circumstances permit. The whole point of socialist politics is to work for people to be able to develop their lives freely on the basis of communal ownership of the means of production. It is true that contemporary conditions do impose political obligations on people, since without politics little can be done on a social scale, and measures have therefore to be taken to see that these obligations are fulfilled. But political life itself is thrown into disarray if politics are so conducted that the political obligations people are urged to accept, or coerced into accepting, are in conflict with what they have learned from experience to consider personal obligations of regard to others.

A fundamental principle of rational value judgment about ends and means, and the subordination of means to ends, is that only persons are ends, and anything else only means. This is entailed, obviously, by the standard of judging the desirability of forms of association by how they promote the human way of life, that is to say, how they serve the lives of persons and not anything else. Thus objects are used as means, and similarly institutions are set up as means. Objects and institutions are only means, not ends—and to regard them as ends is a logical absurdity and a moral atrocity. It means subordinating living people, who feel and think, to material things and social institutions which do neither. What it amounts to is symbolised in the well-known festival of the juggernaut: living people throw themselves down before and are crushed by the great juggernaut—which is itself built and pushed along by people.

The principal ideological alienation effect of private property consists of thinking of people as means and of objects and institutions as ends. Thus as Marx and Engels observed in *The German Ideology*, "in all ideology men and their circumstances appear upside down". For instead of objects being fashioned and institutions instituted to serve people, it appears that people must devote their lives to seeking values embodied in objects and be bound by institutions which exact service for their own sakes. As Marx and Engels added, "this phenomenon arises just as much from their historical life process as the inversion of objects on the retina does from their physical life process".

With private appropriation goes the development of commodity production, which profoundly affects the way people think of values—as is shown in customary uses of words. Objects made, exchanged and used are called and thought of as "goods" and "values". This use of language and way of thinking expresses the fact that people have to devote themselves to producing and appropriating objects, which are themselves the values they seek after (or their equivalent in money), rather than the enjoyment of human activity itself. Human activity is for the sake of objects, rather than objects being valued for their use in human activity. This is what Marx (*Capital*, I, 1, 4) termed "the fetishism of commodities". And this upside down way of looking at things, in which objects are the goods and values, results in people being valued in the way commodities are. Thus if businessmen are discussing whom to appoint to manage a new factory, they may conclude: "Smith is a good man". They value the man (in terms of both use-value and exchange-value) in the same way as they value the products.

Having adopted a way of living by appropriating and exchanging objects, and having thus made objects into values to the production and acquisition of which human life is devoted, people have to associate themselves into distinct and rival communities, of which the modern nation is the most highly developed example, and institute states and all manner of organisations, in order to enable the mode of production, appropriation and exchange to be carried on. These organisations or institutions then exact service. When objects are turned into values, so that people are subordinated to objects, and value each other like objects, the result is also that people see their obligations as owed, not simply to other people, but to organisations. Organisations and institutions likewise become ends, and not mere means.

On the basis of private property and commodity production, then, from which emerges that way of speaking and thinking for which objects are "goods" and "values", there emerges also the way of speaking and thinking for which particular communities, institutions and organisations have a being of their own, with their own interests and requirements, independent of and superior to that of individual people, and imposing claims on them. This is, indeed, the source of that whole verbal procedure of making abstractions into concrete things (the so-called "hypostatisation" or "reification", that is, "thingification", of abstractions) which is enshrined in religion, developed in metaphysical and idealist ways of thinking in general, and issues in so many very peculiar uses of language that set unanswerable conundrums to philosophers.

The entire upside-down world we have made for ourselves needs putting right side up. In practice, this means achieving the communist mode of productive association in which economic activity is planned for providing for the satisfaction

54

of human needs—in which, in the words of ?
Manifesto, "all production is concentrated in the
vast association . . . an association in which the free
ment of each is the condition for the free development
And in ideas, it means arriving at rational value judgmen.
which means are not presented as ends, and only persons
their activities are ends.

The communist aim of a desirable form of human association
is, of course, economic. For what is or is not attainable by
people does depend on the economic organisation of society.
At the same time, an aim which was exclusively economic,
which only consisted in advocating a certain form of economic
activity, would obviously be abstract and incomplete, since
economic activity is not the whole of life but only its necessary
basis, and not an end but a means. In a society in which the
use of modern techniques is developed and planned on the
basis of communal ownership, productive work ceases to be
arduous or time-consuming. In such a society people must
make arrangements to provide themselves with all-round
education, to equip themselves with knowledge, mental and
manual skills and culture, and to provide themselves with all
the opportunities and incentives to develop all-round individual abilities and capacity to enjoy leisure and free activity.
The communist aim includes all that, and this is the practical
content of the slogan, "From each according to his abilities, to
each according to his needs". Economic activity and economic
organisation is for the sake of the development of the personal
capacities, relations, needs and satisfactions of needs, and
enjoyments, of individual people.

What, then, of that "free development of human energy
which is an end in itself"?

In the totality of individual human activities which make up
social life each person and his activity is always dependent on
and contributory to other persons and their activity, so that
while only persons and their activities are ends, no such end is
ever exclusively an end in itself but always at the same time
a means to other ends. However satisfying any one activity

results may be to the individual or individuals concerned,
always, when viewed in relation to the wider field of social
and to other individuals and other activities, done or
ieved not only for its own sake but for the sake of some-
ing else—just as no single person could ever exist, or any
ersonal activity be enjoyed, unless supported and sustained
by other persons and other activities.

But in the communist conception of social ends, the development of the totality of personal activities, as distinct from
particular activities within it, is not advocated for the sake of
anything else, but for its own sake. And here is the only
absolute in human evaluation.

11

Freedom, Necessity and Obligation

The communist form of association, made practical and desirable by men's technological progress, is one in which the end of association becomes, in Marx's phrase, the "free development of human energies". The satisfaction of individual needs is a means to this end. For human needs are the needs for human life, and life is activity of individual organisms. The communist aim is, then, for people to associate to supply the needs of each individual, so that in doing so, and as a result of it, each may enjoy along with and in his dependence on others the free exercise and development of his individual human capacities.

This end is expressed, not just as "development", but as "free development", for the simple reason that in so far as people are constrained or coerced in what they do they are being treated as means and their development and enjoyment of life as persons is distorted and frustrated. The word "free", in this context, therefore carries the negative significance of "not coerced or constrained". An activity is freely done when a person chooses to do it and carries it through without external constraint. A person is free in so far as he is not coerced in his choice of activity and is allowed to do what he chooses to do.

On the other hand, those definitions of "freedom" (such as that proposed by Hegel in his political philosophy) which suggest that individuals are only free when regimented by the state, represent only a gross misuse of words for the purpose of calling unfreedom by the honorific name of freedom. The usual apology for such definitions is that the individual can truly be said to be free only when directed for his own good in a way that effectively prevents the domination of his behaviour by his own unfree irrational individual impulses. The free person, however, directs his own impulses for himself, and does not need to be himself subjected for his own good to the impulsive behaviour of policemen.

Evidently, freedom is a possession of individuals. Just as every social attribute is derivative from the activities and relations of individuals, so is freedom. A free society is an association providing for individual freedom. And to the extent that individuals lack freedom their society falls short of being a free society.

Freedom exists only in the persons of definite individuals, and then only in their carrying out definite activities. To speak, therefore of freedom in general, as a condition or as an aim, and to say in general terms that people or society are free or not free, is to use words vaguely and ambiguously in a way that may cover up a variety of negations of freedom (and very often does, as in the contemporary expression "the free world"). It is necessary to say which persons are free, and in what respects, and to do what. In the course of social development (in which alone both freedom and unfreedom occur) men have made themselves free in various respects and in various relationships and, at the same time, enslaved one another in other respects and in other relationships.

The scope of human freedom, in the sense of the variety of activities men are capable of successfully undertaking, is always conditioned by the actual physical constitution of the human body but is the product of technological progress. The invention of technological means and the subduing of natural forces for human ends provides the basis, and the greater the technological proficiency of men the greater is the scope of the freedom attainable by individuals. Thus in primitive societies, although within the communal relations men are comparatively free from coercion and subjection to one another, their technological backwardness places them in a comparatively subject position to nature. There is not much any individual can do outside the round of traditional tribal activities they all do together, and consequently the whole idea of their being individuals with rights and interests of their own does not occur to people. The "noble savage" was only thought to be free by bourgeois romantics, he does not think of himself as a free individual. Consciousness, as Marx and Engels put it (*The German Ideology*, I, 1), remains "mere herd-consciousness". On the other hand, as people have developed their technology and mastery over nature they have made themselves subject to each other. Thus there develops a contradiction between the actual scope of freedom made possible by technological development, and the opportunities which their social relations offer to individuals of benefiting from it. Class struggles accordingly take on the conscious aspect of struggles for freedom—not for freedom in general, but for specific freedoms—as people denied opportunities contend for them, and others combine to defend those freedoms, in the form of privileges, which they have got at the expense of the former. Capitalism, vehicle of revolutionary technological advance, has allowed extended freedom to be won for individuals, as the under-privileged classes have contended for opportunities of enjoyment and advantage. Although up to the present modern industry has tied people to machines, it is by its productivity the agency of freedom. Its fullest development and use provides for fullest individual freedom. The communist form of association, corresponding to the requirements of the unfettered development and use of modern technology, provides the basis for and serves the end of the maximum enlargement of the scope of human freedom and the enjoyment of free activity by all individuals.

The exercise of free activity is subject to necessary conditions, without which it could not take place. For the unfrustrated enjoyment of freedom, therefore, in any conscious activity, people have consciously to submit themselves to its necessary conditions—to know what they are, and to observe them. In any sphere of activity, freedom entails appreciation of necessity. And this necessity is expressed in negative and conditional generalisations, of the form: "So and so never happens, or cannot be done", "So and so never happens, or cannot be done, without so and so".

In the first place, the carrying through of any undertaking

59

depends on the causal properties of the subject of the undertaking and of the instruments used—including, under the latter heading, the human body itself. It was in this connection that Engels (*Anti-Duhring*, chapter 11) originally said that "freedom consists in the control over ourselves and over external nature which is founded on knowledge of natural necessity". His point was that ourselves and everything else being subject to causal determination does not prohibit the possibility of our free action but is its condition. If *anything* could happen, then we could not make anything happen according to our own intentions. And the more we know about the causal laws which we cannot alter, the more free we are to produce the effects we want. When, after more than fifty years, the same point percolated through to bourgeois philosophy, the eminent "linguistic" philosopher Professor Ryle remarked that the fact that both billiard balls and billiard players are subject to the laws of mechanics does not prohibit the free play of billiards but is its necessary condition.

To win and realise freedom in human activity, therefore, it is in the first place necessary to appreciate that it is in all respects subject to causal law, and to get to know as much about that law as possible. Such knowledge is a condition for enlarging the scope of our freedom. It is in the second place necessary to appreciate the conditions which must be satisfied in the sphere of human relations. For individuals, the necessity of these conditions, when clearly appreciated, takes the form of obligations. The appreciation of necessity in the form of obligations is, then, a condition for extending and universally realising the actual enjoyment of freedom.

The basic obligation of freedom in communist association is simply the obligation to work. For as Marx observed (*Capital*, III, 48, 3), work must be done, and however much labour is lightened and made interesting and attractive, however short the necessary working hours, and however wide the choice of occupation, it "still remains a realm of necessity". It is indeed, as he said elsewhere (*Critique of the Gotha Programme*), "the prime necessity of life".

In order to be able to work, and then to be able to enjoy the advantages and opportunities afforded by the products of work, human individuals are dependent on one another, and upon their complex social association, in a variety of ways. Indeed, no individual can ever do much without the good will of others. In general, then, individuals who are to enjoy freedom of activity must necessarily work together and then, both in their working relations and in all their consequent relations, they must require of each other and give to each other support, sympathy and consideration.

These necessary conditions in the regulation of human behaviour, that is, the behaviour of individuals, which constitute the obligations necessary for the enjoyment of free personal activity, are summed up in the so-called "golden rule"—treat others as you would have them treat you. You would have them work for you, so you must work for them; you would have them minister to your needs, so you must minister to theirs; you would have them be kind, sympathetic and considerate to you, so you must be so to them; you would not have them use you to your disadvantage in order to get something for themselves, so you must not use them in such a way. This rule was attributed to the legendary Christ; it is simply the expression of the experience and practical wisdom of those who work together. But it has never been practised on any wide scale because (as Jesus himself was reported to have pointed out) it is totally impracticable in societies based on private property.

In communist society, when the practical relations between individuals have become "perfectly intelligible and reasonable", social obligation becomes simply what is necessary as the condition for enjoying free activity on the basis of working together. As moral words are now generally used, the words "must" and "must not" are often and unthinkingly used as synonymous for "ought" and "ought not". In communist society "ought" has no other significance than the ordinary conditional "must". Obligations are simply what everyone must accept in order to carry on their associated free activity, just as, in a related sense, they must accept the laws of nature in order to carry on their intercourse with nature. A person who behaves badly has then to be treated as one who has made a mistake (possibly a very serious one, but only a mistake none the less) which others will take it upon themselves to correct in him—just as someone who makes some mistake at work would be corrected by his fellows. Morality altogether ceases to be something socially *imposed* on individuals as a *restriction* of their activity. And as to all those activities which men and women enjoy together as friends and lovers, and which constitute the principal element in their individual happiness—these do not come within "the realm of necessity" but of free activity, made possible by the mutual fulfilment of obligations.

In a communist society questions of morality, private and public, would become perfectly intelligible—for questions of "ought" would become questions of "must", and it would be as obvious that we must not set out to violate the golden rule of human relations as that we must not try to violate the laws of nature: in either case we could not get what we wanted. But where people are still divided, having to use one another as means and subject themselves to their own means of production, to their own products and to their own institutions and organisations, moral standards cannot but appear as *impositions* and, moreover, the contradictions in human relations are reflected in contradictions in standards and in obligations. In so far as human relations fall short of intelligibility and rationality, so must human morality.

12

Morality

As hitherto recommended, morality has always been an external imposition on individuals. And that is because, as words are commonly understood, the question "Why ought I to do this?" is distinct from the question "What will I get out of it?" To be guided only by considerations of personal preference and advantage is the negation of morality. And consequently it is always open to the individual to ask "Why should I be moral at all? And if I am, why should I follow this prescription rather than some contrary one?" In conditions when some moral code has been so thoroughly implanted in people that they never question it, such questions, naturally, do not arise. But in the present transitional state of society they are asked by many people and worry them a great deal.

From the time of Thomas Hobbes, those bourgeois moralists who rejected theories of a supernatural origin and supernatural sanctions for morality have in many cases accepted it as an axiom that people are so constituted as always to seek their own advantage, or their own satisfactions, or (as it used to be expressed) pleasures. Obviously, as Hobbes already pointed out, if everyone seeks only his own advantage, without regard to anyone else, the results must be chaotic and to the advantage of nobody. Puzzling this out led to the utilitarian principle, that morality consists of precepts designed to regulate individual actions in such a way as to make for the greatest advantage, or the greatest possible sum of satisfactions, for everyone.

There is an obvious snag in the utilitarian principle of basing the morality of actions on the advantages or satisfactions to be gained from them. It is that such satisfactions belong only to individuals, not to communities, and in many cases the advantage to be gained by individuals by acting against the precepts of morality is greater than that to be gained by obeying them. It is not true that it always pays to be good. But if the only basis for morality is the gaining of satisfactions, how persuade the individual to forgo satisfactions for the sake of morality, or for the sake of the satisfactions of others, when he knows that many others decline to forgo their satisfactions for the sake of his? Recognising this difficulty, Jeremy Bentham (the most practical and consistent and, therefore, also the most objectionable of all bourgeois moralists) made it his life's work to exhort the legislature to devise laws to ensure that bad people should never get what they wanted. People will never be moral unless in some way bullied or frightened into it. Jeremy Bentham thought (and with some justification) that to make working people, for example, forgo the pleasures of idleness and shoulder the moral task of industry it would be more efficacious to legislate for starvation and build workhouses than merely to encourage Wesleyan Methodism and threaten them with hell fire.

For even the most naturalistic bourgeois ethics, therefore, morality turns out to be just as much an external imposition on individuals as it is for more spiritual-minded accounts of it. Derive it from material pleasures and satisfactions or from God and the angels—morality is still a thing alien to and imposed on individuals.

This state of affairs is not difficult to account for. Human society is based on the social production of the means of life, and people's association in society, within which alone they become persons, must always assume some definite form, determined by the mode of production and expressed in their property relations. The form of association determines corresponding moral obligations, in as much as its maintenance and development requires standards of how people should live and behave and treat one another. Moral obligations are then what persons owe to each other on account of their social association. This means that obligations entail rights, which are simply the converse of obligations. If each person has duties to others, they have duties to him—and that constitutes his personal claim on them, or his rights. These conceptions develop and change with the development and change of the form of association. And, naturally, in associations in which different persons are considered as having different social status, obligations and rights are not uniform for all persons. Some persons have more rights and fewer obligations, and others more obligations and fewer rights.

There is and can be no such thing as human association "in general" but only particular forms of association, to which different prescriptive conceptions of obligations and rights correspond. Where there are class divisions and one class interest is dominant within the given form of association, the corresponding obligations and rights express the dominant class interest, and the corresponding moral code becomes class-biased, not a code of universal but of class-biased morality. And then where class interests are in conflict, and where also the private interests of individuals are in conflict with proclaimed social obligations, it is impossible that any obligations should be generally fulfilled or rights respected without being in some measure enforced. Consequently the assertion of obligations and rights, necessary in human association, has to be effected by socially organised means of moral exhortation, persuasion and pressure backed by physical coercion and the exaction of penalties.

It may be concluded that so long as private property, with its divisive effects, continues to form the basis of human association, morality must always take the form of a moral code socially imposed on individuals—and moreover of a code which, while claiming universality, is in reality a disguised expression of class interest. The whole long effort of bourgeois radicals to make morality acceptable to all individuals as being in all their interests is itself merely an ideological product of the bourgeois property relations. For the whole concept of "advantage", "interest", "satisfaction" and "pleasure", on which they try to base morality, is generated from private property—since it makes the good or end something you get or appropriate, and not something you do. And it founders hopelessly on the divisive effects of private property.

But whatever the theory of ethics, the moral code never appears under an amiable or sympathetic aspect. Whether it appears in the starry raiment of Wordsworth's "Stern Daughter of the Voice of God" or in the more earthy habiliments of a Benthamite workhouse master, its accent is always stern and its aspect forbidding.

Not only does morality, as Lucretius said of religion, present an alien face "glowering at mortal men", but its deliverances are so contradictory that the person trying to live a moral life often does not know what to make of them. As well as being presented with contradictions in standards of judgment and assessment of what is praiseworthy or blameworthy, which are inevitable products of a society in which there are basic conflicts of class and sectional interest, there are no standards of judgment and assessment which yield unambiguous instructions. For example, when both thrift and generosity are virtues, and meanness and extravagance vices, how find the path of virtue and avoidance of vice? Or when obeying authority and consideration for others are both duties, what to do when the instructions of authority are inconsiderate or cruel? It is for these reasons that Aristotle said long ago that virtue was "the golden mean", and later Protestant and bourgeois moralists said that each man was responsible to himself and must follow "the monitor within"—and then denounced those whose inner monitors pronounced instructions they objected to. Today existentialist sages conclude that all choices are morally agonising and one has simply to choose.

These and similar moral contradictions arise from the fact that people see their end or good in the appropriation and possession of objects, see their obligations to one another in the form of obligations to institutions, and treat one another as objects and as means to the production and appropriation of objects. The basic contradiction lies in the fact that no one can then regard others in the same way as he regards himself (and this, no doubt, is also a reason why, in the most sophisticated bourgeois philosophy, the existence of other people as persons like oneself becomes problematic). For whereas

66

people—other people—are regarded as objects and mere means, one can never regard oneself like that. The universalisability and consistency of moral judgments entails the application of the golden rule, but so long as people are so associated as to treat each other as things it can never be consistently applied. Thus moral judgments, which are meant to be universalisable, can never in practice be universalised. There are always moral contradictions and conflicts.

At the same time there has continually been asserted the idea that human relations should be governed by human sympathy, in defiance of all property, all authority and all moral codes. The perennial human conflict is between the expression and application of this idea and the demands made upon people by their economic relations and their institutions. This idea arises from amidst the masses of the working people, and has been eloquently expressed through the ages by poets, prophets, artists and philosophers; the conflict occurs in individual life, in the class struggle, in politics, religion, the arts, philosophy and, indeed, in every department of human activity. So long, however, as the contradictions of real life are not scientifically laid bare, the ideal of human relations seems to come "from the heart" rather than from reason, and to be a sentiment and aspiration rather than a practical programme of social reconstruction. But scientific humanism unites the human heart and human reason. The sentiments of the heart are fully expressed by the voice of reason.

Under communism, morality as an externally imposed restraint on free personal activity disappears, along with its ugly sister products of alienation—the state, politics and religion. For then there are no grounds for maintaining a state organisation to govern people, or engaging in politics to assert particular interests in the state. There are no grounds for imagining people to be lost in their material environment and sunk in sin, depending on supernatural agencies for their salvation. And the form of human association corresponds to individual needs and imposes on individuals no obligations that need be enforced on them contrary to the enjoyment of their free activity. When there are no longer conflicts of interest rooted in the ways people appropriate objects for their use, and when consequently there is no contradiction between how one would want others to treat oneself and how it is in one's interests to treat them, then self-knowledge and human sympathy can become the guide in life, and the golden rule of human relations can at last apply.

13

Morals and Politics of Class Struggle

The social development through which men make their way towards conditions of freedom involves and always has involved consciously conducted struggle, of men against intractable forces of nature and natural obstacles to human desires, and also of men against men. The former have made men adventurous and inured against various forms of hardship, the latter have made them cruel and vengeful and indifferent to the sufferings of others. As a result of developing language and conceptual thought, and so becoming aware of themselves and each other as persons, with common aims and dependent on each other, men have developed those traits of mutual regard and behaviour which are expressed by the word "humanity". And from exactly the same source, conjoined with the socially produced conflicts between them, they have developed the traits of "inhumanity". These are polar opposites emerging in the same process of human development, and the one could not emerge without the other. Thus if love, friendship, laughter and pity, products of human consciousness, are qualities foreign to the rest of the animal world and assume the form of human values, so is man's inhumanity to man a quality foreign to other animals, assuming the form of human evil. In our present epoch, with the advance of socialised co-operative production and the equalisation of persons, the values of humanity have become more prized than ever before, and are given practical expression in such things as the development of medicine, education and the social services. At the same time it has produced, and continues to produce, far more monstrous evidences of inhumanity than any previous epoch. The same technical resources which enable the one to be practised on a large scale do the same for the other.

To pretend, in the arena of human conflicts, that the precepts of humanity can become the universal guide of behaviour, is simply to close one's eyes to the actual human situation. If conflicts are there, it is impossible to contract out of them. And if any good is to come out of them they must be fought to a finish, and that means that men must go on inflicting injury on men. The Christian precept of "meekness" was advice given to poor men in circumstances when there was no visible prospect of their emancipation—but if "the meek shall inherit the earth" they cannot be meek in claiming their inheritance.

It is perhaps no wonder that in the conduct of class struggle, both in public policy and in individual conduct, actions occur and recur that can only be understood as products of the still inhuman condition of humanity, in which human relations are not yet intelligible and reasonable. For William Morris spoke the simple truth when he stated, at the conclusion of a lecture on *Communism*, "that any other state of society but communism is grievous and disgraceful to all belonging to it", and that action within the present state of society could never escape the taint of its conditions. The communist will not on that account give up the struggle and talk about "the god that failed", but persevere; and continue to say, as Morris said in the same lecture: "Intelligence enough to conceive, courage enough to will, power enough to compel. If our ideas of a new society are anything more than a dream, these three qualities must animate the due effective majority of the working people; and then, I say, the thing will be done."

Until all exploitation of man by man is ended, morality cannot be based on a generalised human standpoint, expressing a common human point of view and interest, but only on a class standpoint. It either accepts a class-divided society without challenge, and then it is the expression of the point of view and interest of the exploiting classes; or it demands the abolition of class divisions, and then it is alien to exploiting classes and expresses the point of view and interest only of the others. The morality of scientific socialism and communism is

70

class-biased and militant, and calls for a fight of all the working classes to overcome, as is now possible, the old and still present conditions of exploitation and alienation. For them, the practicability and human desirability of the aim demands and justifies the adoption of all those means of organised struggle which are necessary for attaining it. That implies that regard for human values must be made effective by opposition to whoever frustrates their realisation, and love and respect for one's fellows by hatred and contempt for those who live at the expense of others.

Having seen through the illusions of religion, with its conviction of sin and reliance on divine help; having understood the issues at stake in class struggle; having understood the functions of constituted state authority and the ideologies that go with it; and having rejected the imposition of a supposedly universal morality, whether it is based on calculations of maximum satisfaction and reconciliation of interests, or on divine revelation—for them the guide for conduct (as opposed to simple considerations of personal advantage) can only be found in considerations of what is demanded for the emancipation of labour.

For individuals, this still remains an imposition. For it opposes demands of social responsibility against individual interests, satisfactions and enjoyments. At the same time, a way of life in which each would live for the sake of his own satisfactions, simply making such adjustments and compromises as he has to in view of the fact that other people exist as well, cannot in fact satisfy, because it is the negation of people's togetherness and interdependence. In application, it deprives the individual of any aim to be achieved in his relations with others, on which relations, nevertheless, the whole mode of existence of himself and all other individuals depends. Such a deprived individual (common in all classes of contemporary society) has, of course, his personal ambitions: what he will get for himself, and what he will get others to get for him. But in the moral sense he is aimless. And when his ambition fails, and when, in any case, death overtakes him, he suffers complete frustration. As the popular saying says, "You can't take it with you". Each individual does need something besides his own satisfactions to live for, because of the way we have to live together, and something, too, besides his own personal possessions (in which category immediate family ties are included). This desideratum is often expressed by saying that we need to find "the meaning" of life, or to give life "a meaning", where the word "meaning" is used in much the same way as "aim", "end" or "purpose". Communism does serve individuals by giving life a meaning—a meaning derived from considerations of the real conditions of human life.